SCHOLASTIC
News
Nonfiction Readers

Snakes and Other Reptiles

by
Mary Schulte

Children's Press®
A Division of Scholastic Inc.
New York Toronto London Auckland Sydney
Mexico City New Delhi Hong Kong
Danbury, Connecticut

These content vocabulary word builders
are for grades 1-2.

Consultant: Dr. Dale Madison
Department of Biological Sciences
Binghamton University
Binghamton, New York

Curriculum Specialist: Linda Bullock

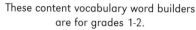

Special thanks to Omaha's Henry Doorly Zoo

Photo Credits:

Photographs © 2005: Bruce Coleman Inc./Alan Bank: 5 bottom right, 14; Corbis Images/Kevin Schafer: cover background; Dan Suzio Photography: 5 top left, 9; Dembinsky Photo Assoc.: 23 bottom left (Jesse Cancelmo), cover left inset (E. R. Degginger), back cover, 5 bottom left, 10, 11 (Skip Moody), 20, 21 (Alan G. Nelson), cover center inset (Gerhard Schulz), 2, 4 bottom right, 7 (A. B. Sheldon); Dwight R. Kuhn Photography: 23 top left; Minden Pictures: 1, 4 bottom left, 12, 15 (Heidi & Hans-Jurgen Koch), 4 top, 17 (Mike Parry); National Geographic Image Collection/Tim Laman: cover right inset, 5 top right, 19; Nature Picture Library Ltd.: 23 top right (Nick Garbutt), 23 bottom right (Barry Mansell); NHPA/Anthony Bannister: 13.

Book Design: Simonsays Design!

Library of Congress Cataloging-in-Publication Data

Schulte, Mary, 1958-
  Snakes and other reptiles / by Mary Schulte.
    p. cm. – (Scholastic news nonfiction readers)
  Includes bibliographical references and index.
  ISBN 0-516-24936-3 (lib. bdg.)
  1. Reptiles–Juvenile literature. I. Title. II. Series.
  QL644.2.S34 2005
  597.9–dc22
                                        2005003298

1 2 3 4 5 6 7 8 9 10 R 14 13 12 11 10 09 08 07 06 05

CONTENTS

WORD HUNT

Look for these words as you read. They will be **bold**.

crocodile
(**krok**-uh-dile)

molt
(mohlt)

reptile
(**rep**-tile)

4

hatch
(hach)

komodo dragon
(kuh-**moh**-doh **drag**-uhn)

scales
(skales)

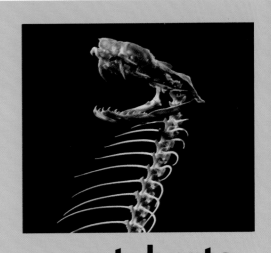

vertebrate
(**vur**-tuh-brate)

Reptiles! Reptiles!

Have you ever seen a turtle, a snake, or a lizard?

All of these animals are **reptiles**.

There are lots of ways you can tell an animal is a reptile.

Turtles are reptiles.

Some reptiles **hatch** from eggs.

Snakes are reptiles. Some of them hatch from eggs.

Snake eggs have a soft shell.

Look! This snake is hatching from its egg.

Reptiles have **scales**.

Scales are hard pieces of skin that protect the reptile's body.

scales

Look at this snake, it's blue!
This is a blue racer snake.

Reptiles **molt**.

This means they shed their skin as they grow.

When snakes molt, they rub off their old skin.

molting

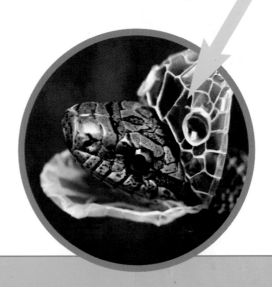

new skin

old skin

Look! This snake has shed its old skin. Now it has new skin.

Reptiles have backbones.

Animals with a backbone are called **vertebrates**.

A snake has a backbone. That means snakes are vertebrates.

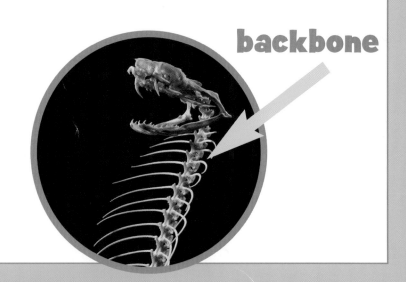

backbone

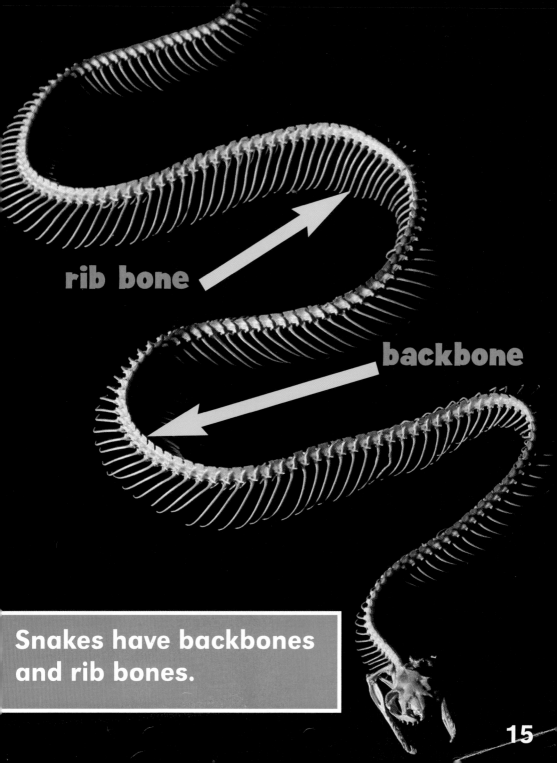

rib bone

backbone

Snakes have backbones and rib bones.

Reptiles live on land and in water.

Crocodiles are reptiles.

They walk on land.

They swim in water.

They come up to the top of the water to breathe air.

This crocodile
is underwater.

Reptiles are cold-blooded.

Their body temperature changes to match the air.

A **komodo dragon** is a reptile.

If the air is cold, the komodo dragon is cold.

If the air is warm, the komodo dragon is warm.

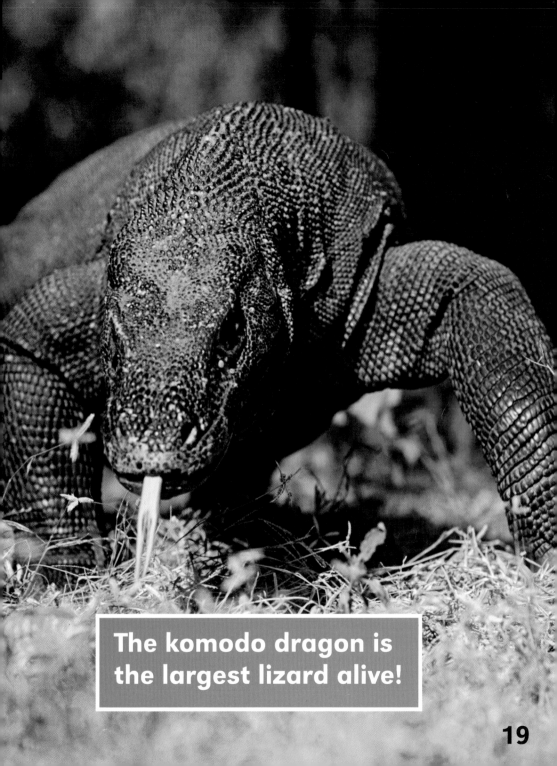

The komodo dragon is
the largest lizard alive!

PARTS OF A REPTILE
Here is an X-ray of a Snake.

backbone

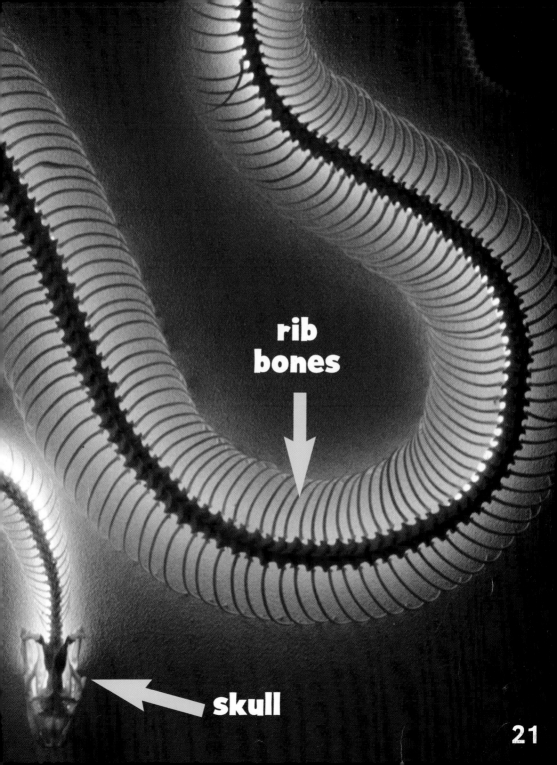

rib
bones

skull

YOUR NEW WORDS

crocodile (**krok**-uh-dile) a reptile with short legs and strong jaws

hatch (hach) to break out of an egg

komodo dragon (kuh-**moh**-doh **drag**-uhn) the largest lizard alive; it lives on its own island

molt (mohlt) to shed the outer layer of skin

reptile (**rep**-tile) a cold-blooded animal with a backbone and scales

scales (skales) hard pieces of skin that cover a reptile and help keep it safe

vertebrate (**vur**-tuh-brate) an animal with a backbone

IS IT A REPTILE?

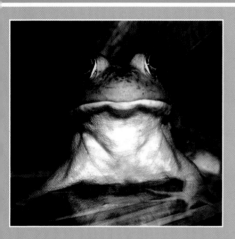

Bullfrog
(No. It's an amphibian.)

Cockroach
(No. It's an insect.)

Eel
(No. It's a fish.)

Salamander
(No. It's an amphibian.)

INDEX

FIND OUT MORE

Book:

Snakes by Maria Mudd Ruth (Marshall Cavendish Corporation, 2002)

Website:

http://cybersleuth-kids.com/sleuth/Science/Animals/Reptiles/

MEET THE AUTHOR:

Mary Schulte is a newspaper photo editor and author of books and articles for children. She is the author of the other animal classification books in this series. She lives in Kansas City, Missouri, where she has seen a garter snake in her garden.